WALKING
MIRACLE

WALKING MIRACLE

*Memoir of a 19-Year-Old
Stroke Survivor*

TICHINA S. TAYLOR
As told to Dr. Nioka Smith

J. Kenkade
PUBLISHING®
Little Rock, Arkansas

Walking Miracle
Copyright © 2019 by Tichina Taylor
Written by Dr. Nioka Smith

J. Kenkade Publishing
6104 Forbing Rd Little Rock, AR 72209
www.jkenkadepublishing.com

J. Kenkade Publishing is a registered trademark.

Printed in the United States of America
ISBN 978-1-944486-68-6

Unless otherwise noted, scripture quotations are taken from the King James Version Bible, Public Domain.

This book recounts actual events in the life of Tichina Taylor according to the author's recollection and perspective. Some of the names and identifying details may have been changed to respect the privacy of those involved.

To everyone reading this book,
God loves you.

ACKNOWLEDGMENTS

I want to thank my mom.

She's feisty, but sweet at the same time. She is the sweetest person I've ever seen, and she follows after God. I love you mom. Thank you for being there. Thank you so much for everything.

To my dad,

I love you. Rest in love. Farewell.

To my brother in law, Coral (Rell),

Thank you for listening to God and being led to return home that day of my stroke. Thank you for finding me and for taking the measures you did to help save my life that day. You're the best.

To my pastors, Apostle Kingsley Eruemulor and Dr. Aleobe Eruemulor,

I thank you for listening to God and for praying for me always. I love you.

To Pastor Catherine Amaka Ikeh,

Thank you for obeying God and telling me to start exercising my right hand.

To everyone who has ever prayed for me, visited me, and sent encouraging words while I was hospitalized and after the stroke, thank you. May God bless you.

TABLE OF CONTENTS

PROLOGUE

Hi, I'm Miracle. That's my nickname since I was a baby. Mama always said I was a miracle baby. She says when I was born, the umbilical cord was wrapped around my neck three times, strangling me when mama pushed. Mama's doctor didn't know quite what to do to deliver me safely and mama was slowly losing me minute by minute. That's when Dr. Hank Mitchell walked in at the nick of time, performed a special emergency caesarean and delivered me safely. Mama stayed in the hospital for five days with me. My daddy told mama to name me Tichina. He said he'd gotten if off of Tichina Arnold, the actress that played Pam on the 90s hit television show "Martin". My dad said that it should be actually pronounced Ti-Chyna, not Ti-Cheena. My sister begged mama to name me Shonte, so mama made that my middle name. So, there was my full name: Tichina Shonte Taylor.

But mama took one look at me, emotional from how I'd almost died and named me "Miracle".

Miracle is my nickname. Only family calls me that though. And only family knows why. My birth wasn't the only miracle. Many events would add more badges to my name Miracle. There were many miracles before the stroke.

1

THE FIRST OF MIRACLES

My mother had just gotten out of my aunt's car to take groceries in the house. She told my brother to grab me out of the car and take me in the house. I was one year old and had just recently learned how to walk. I'm not sure if my brother heard my mom or not, but he walked in the house without me. A few minutes later, I walked out of the car on my own.

"Ahhhhh!" My sister screamed frantically.

"Aunt Vicky!" Ahhhh! Tichina…car…Mama!"

My sister was lost for words as she tried to tell my Aunt that she had just hit me, knocked me down, and now my little body was completely under the body of her Oldsmobile.

As my aunt drove backwards out of the drive-way trying to decipher my sister's words and screams, I became trapped under her car.

I was only one year old, and my auntie had run over me in her car! Yes—I was completely under her car. I say run over, but I only had a scratch. All the tires missed me, and I was only hit by the bumper on my head.

And this would mark the second badge added to my name Miracle for this was the second miracle God provided in my life.

When I hear my mom and siblings tell me the stories now about my miracles, I just sit back and listen. My mom and siblings tell me all the time about the few times my mom was riding on the highway and I literally fell out of the car. Yep! Right onto the highway with other cars behind me. I'd definitely say that was another miracle that none of those cars ever touched me. I know without a doubt God was sending his angels all around me.

What was it with those cars?!

I say I don't know why the enemy wanted me out of here so badly, but he surely never gave up. Mama was a praying woman! I've been blessed by her prayers for as young as I can remember. I can remember them being as loud and as strong as the rumbles and the whistles of the train around the corner. Her prayers got through to Heaven's gates for me! My daddy and sister had given me a name, but mama, Oh, she *knew* what to name me. And these were the first of miracles for me!

2

NORMAL

I never really got sick at all before the stroke. Maybe a cough here and there, but never really sick. I was definitely a healthy child. In fact, when I was born, everyone said I looked like one of those fat Chinese babies. My cheeks were so huge! My eyes were so tight that they literally disappeared when I smiled. That still makes me laugh today!

I look back at my baby pictures and I ask my mom, "Gheez! What did you eat when you were pregnant with me?"

My mom responds back and says, "Fruit. Lots of fruit."

And I say, "Was the fruit injected with meat?"

My life was pretty good as a kid. I was the baby, so you know what that means? I kind of got my way *a lot*. I was everyone's "China Doll".

My grandmother named me that and everyone sort of gravitated to that nickname. When I was born, my grandmother looked at me and said, "I'm going to call her my China Doll! Still to this day, she calls me China Doll. Growing up, I didn't have any cousins my age, so I was pretty lonely...*a lot*. For fun, I'd ride my bike outside by myself. I'd watch SpongeBob and Hey Arnold on television, and pry into my big sister's business, listen in on her phone calls, and invite myself in the room when her friends were over.

You know, normal stuff!

I was so excited when a new girl my age named Katrice moved right next door to me. We instantly became best friends! We went to the same school and were in the same class. We did normal things little elementary kids do such as fight over little things, break up as friends, and then become besties again, talk about who likes who, who doesn't like who, polish our nails, and create dance routines to the latest new songs such as "It's Getting Hot in Herre" by Nelly.

Oops. Were we supposed to be listening to that?

Yea, that brings me to my mom. The television station, BET, was banned in our house. My mom never let us watch it. My mom is a devout Chris-

tian whose relationship with God is the closest
I've ever seen. Going to church in our house was
not an option or a choice. I remember one time
my brother was sick and my mom said, "Come
on, let's go to church. Jesus heals. There's healing
in God's house." Mama was a praying woman!
I remember she always said I was going to be
a prayer warrior. I never really knew what she
meant or when it would happen. I just knew if
a prayer warrior meant that you pray like my
mother, that meant I had a long way to go!

I was involved in praise dancing as a young
girl and teenager. I loved it and I was good at it!
It was a certain beauty about praising God with
your body movement. My legs moved seamlessly,
and my arms would flow with such grace!

When I was younger, I could stand on my toes
without point shoes. I could literally walk on my
toes without ever bending them and everyone
was wowed at my skill. They all said I should be
in ballet classes. I never joined though. I guess
I didn't quite see how special my talent was or
even know that it was a talent back then. I was a
little girl and was just doing what my body could
naturally do. Normal for me, not so normal for
the average Jo. My sister told me I should be a
ballerina. Man, if I could go back to the moment

when I could stand on my toes—or what I would do to even be able to stand with both legs straight right now. I'd probably do just about anything to have that feeling again. The experience of being "normal." Just to be able to walk without a limp, or to run.

Run. I remember that—what it feels like to be able to run. When I was young, people always said how fast I could run. They were literally signing me up for track in their heads. I never joined though. I could outrun anybody in my class with those little legs of mine. I loved to run. I'd run for no reason. My friends and I used to play "red light, yellow light" and I'd be to the finish line before they could say stop.

Yes. That was my normal. Extraordinary to others, but at that time, it was normal to me.

As a little child, I saw a lot of adults and children who were disabled. I'd see people in wheelchairs, those that couldn't talk, those that could barely walk, and I'd secretly say, "Lord, please don't ever let that happen to me." I always felt remorseful for them. It always touched my heart, but if I can be honest, I always prayed that it never happened to me. I was normal. Normal as I knew it.

I went to an elementary school called Excellence Academy where I was in school all the way until 5:30 in the evening! Man, it seemed like I'd never get out of school. In the winter days, it was dark when I got home. I used to struggle in math and my older sister helped tutor me. Probably like half the kids in the world, I hated math! But oh, how I loved to write! Mainly poetry. English class is where I excelled at! It's also where I learned that I was ambidextrous. Yep! I could write with both my right hand and my left hand! That meant a lot to me because as my right hand got tired, I continued to write my poetry with my left hand. This would prove to come in handy years later, after the stroke.

I had grown to love my school and the friends I met. I even had friends at our church.

I was living a great normal life until the summer before my eighth grade school year when my mom decided to pack us up and move us from West Helena, Arkansas to Little Rock, Arkansas. I was so furious! Just like a normal twelve-year-old, my main concern was friends. Moving to Little Rock meant I would lose all of my friends. I didn't want to talk to anybody. I was upset at my mom and my sister because in my mind, she was the reason we were moving up there! She lived in Little Rock and because of her, my mom had this grand idea to move there too! I blamed my sister for losing my friends.

Clementine Middle School. Eighth grade year. Going from a charter school to a public school like that was like a culture shock to me! Those kids didn't care what they said to the teachers. It was like the movie "Lean on Me" all over again! I met some great new friends there though, eventually. I had these two friends named Naomi and Serena. We were really close. I was always the goofy friend. I loved it. I was the one that always laughed at everything. I was usually happy and like most teenage girls, talking on the telephone was my hobby.

When I got to High School the next year, I had begun to settle in to Little Rock. My ninth-grade best friend was Erin. She lived close to our high school. We went over each other's house all the time. We were both foodies, so we went out to eat frequently. My social life was starting to look great now. The move to Little Rock wasn't so bad after all. Shhh. Don't tell my sister!

Erin and I frequented the skating rink. She was the one who introduced me to skating. I had never skated before, but I soon found out that I loved skating! It's funny how we take those little things for granted. Erin and I used to go on

Friday nights because that's when everyone else went. We skated, but mainly, we danced to the hottest new dance line songs such as "Step in the Name of Love." Whenever our favorites songs came on, my friends and I screamed and started dancing! We had so much fun together!

There was this boy named Greg that I used to have a crush on in high school. I remember being at the skating rink with my friend Erin and she was trying to get me to go talk to him and I wouldn't. Then, being the fun bubbly friend that she was, she yelled out "Heyyyy Greg," then looked at me as a way to place his attention on me. I hated her for that, but I thanked her for it because Greg started looking at me from across that skating rink floor and then skated over to me and said the words I was praying he'd say: "Hey Tichina."

Hey Tichina.

That's all he said. But no one could see what he really said with his eyes. Only he and I knew. And from that night, we started talking on the phone all the time. Greg was such a gentleman. We grew very close together, then we grew apart the next year. I don't know. We just stopped talking as much. I guess that happens, but we still remained friends.

I started experiencing some heartbreak later in my senior year. What girl hasn't, huh? Poetry became my outlet. I used to write poetry all the time in high school and I just stopped. In tenth grade though, I thought I was Maya Angelou in my head! I couldn't be stopped. I found a poetry club to go to and became more motivated by the spoken word. I even got a chance to recite my poem at an organization one night and won second place! I was so proud of myself! I was using a gift that God had given me. A gift of writing and speaking. Everybody in the audience was moved by my poem and I received a standing ovation! It makes me understand why the devil came after me so much.

I was using a gift that God had given me. I received a standing ovation! It makes me understand why the devil came after me so much.

In high school, I joined a nonprofit girls group called "Dynamic Girls". It was sort of like a girl talk group where other girls my age and I were able to talk about our pain and experiences. We talked about our everyday life at school and at home and I found a place of familiarity there. It felt like home. I was finding myself. Becoming "Tichina". Acknowledging "Shonte". Evolving

"Miracle".

I was using my gifts, coming out of my shell, and reaching toward greatness. High school came with several opportunities that I took advantage of. Erin tried out for the drill team and encouraged me to try out. I was hesitant at first, but I went ahead and tried out. Unfortunately, I didn't make it. I just couldn't keep up! Those girls were moving it! And shaking it! And dropping it! And by the time they cycled back to shaking it, I was still trying to move it!

The coaches didn't want to leave anyone out who had signed up for the drill team, so they said we could join pep squad instead. I guess they felt sorry for us! So funny!

So, I became one of the newest members of the pep squad! Homecoming night, I finally got the entire dance routine down to a tee. One of my close male friends, Andre, said, "Bout time, Tichina! You're doing something right!" I laughed so hard. I know some people would have been offended, but I wasn't. I told you: I was always the goofy friend. I could laugh at myself when something was true and not be offended by it! I knew I wasn't the best on the pep squad, but I promise you I was having fun! That was me! That was Tichina. That was Miracle. And it was true:

I messed up on all the fast songs. But hey! If you gave me a dance routine to a slow song, oh, I was getting it!

I was a normal teenager whose hobbies included talking on the telephone and going to the movies. And just like every other teenager, friends and boys were the highlight of my life. I was cool with the popular students and the geeks. I got along with everybody. I thought it was crucial to keep up with the hottest fashion trends and hairstyles. I blushed at male attention like other teenage girls such as that one time my friends and I were at lunch walking around in our matching jackets with the bedazzle and fur. After we finished eating our dry cafeteria burgers and stale French fries, we got up from the lunch table and started walking outside to the court. That's when a clique of boys walked up to us.

"I see y'all with your matching jackets on! Dang, you look the hottest Tichina!" I could feel my cheeks expanding to the size of that fluffy Chinese baby I once was. My eyes (or shall I say my mascara) began blinking so fast that I'd miss my moment to speak.

Stop blinking Tichina and talk! Say something! Hi. Thank you. Something. He is about to think you're a lunatic!

"Tichina. Tichina. TICHINA!"

My friend, Crystal was screaming my name, but I couldn't hear her.

All I heard was "Tichina, you look the hottest!"

I heard that like ten times, but I'm pretty sure he only actually said it once!

"Thank you, Matthew," I said as I parted my lips, raised my right shoulder, and tilted my head slightly to the side in a blushing kind of way.

I normally wouldn't pause like that when I liked a guy. And responding was something I never struggled with. But Matthew was different. I was normal. A normal teenager with puppy love. And just like every other teenager who's made a bad decision at least once in their lives, I, too, made some bad decisions. Sort of like those cool jackets my friends and I wore that day to school—umm, yea, they were stolen.

My friends and I had stolen them from this place called the "The Latest Fashion Boutique." You see, Middleton High School had an open campus lunch policy. Only, the principals and teachers didn't know that though. I'm laughing hilariously now as I write this.

Wow! That was bad. The students used to leave campus on lunch as if we really had an open campus policy. There was this school on the other side of town (*the good neighborhood school*) that was able to leave campus on lunch.

Well, we made our own policy:

We pay the school's security officers to let us leave campus on lunch. We swear to never tell administration that they let us do it. If we get caught, it's on us! Security officers look out for us. They guard the doors to ensure no one sees us leave campus. Then, we call or text them when we're on our way back so that they can let us back in to the school with no penalties and no questions asked.

We thought the security officers were the coolest in the world back then. But now when I look back on it, that probably jeopardized our safety in more ways than one! Well, during this particular student-imposed open campus policy, my friends and I left the school campus on our lunch break as we often did. However, this time, instead of going to "The Burger Joint", we went to "The Latest Fashion Boutique" and saw these jackets that were *bomb!* My friends and I screamed.

We just had to have them!

They had fur around the collar and bling down the jacket. The same jackets we had on when Matthew approached me at lunch that day. We were drooling over them and the next thing I know, my friend Jamika said, "Let's take them! Nobody's watching. Hurry up!"

All the time while we were stealing, I was thinking in my head, "I shouldn't be stealing."

I was bad that one year. That *whole* year. The reason I chose to change my circle of friends still baffles me today. Rhonda and Jamika were bad influences. Their names were always in something and they were always getting in trouble. At the time, I didn't think much about it. I would have never stolen anything before I started hanging out with them. I guess that was my rebellious year. But after thinking about it, I snapped back to reality and stopped hanging with them.

Erin and I had lost touch. She was a great friend. My best friend. But we had stopped talking so much. It was time for us to become close friends again because I missed her so much.

"Hey Erin! I miss you so much. What have you been up to?" I screamed with excitement to my best friend. Erin didn't respond. I knew Erin better than this. I know she wasn't a petty person and knew she missed me too.

But for a split second, I thought, "Oh no! Is she mad at me for hanging with that bad clique of girls?"

Erin always wanted the best for me. She was a

true friend. One that would never have encouraged me to steal or skip school. But as I looked at her a little longer, I knew that couldn't be it. That wasn't her character.

"Erin. Erin!" She still didn't respond. She didn't even look up. That's when I realized something was wrong with Erin.

"Erin?" I said with a worried voice. No response.

As I walked over to Erin where her head was against the locker, I pulled on her shoulder, hinting for her to look up at me. I noticed tears running down her face and her eyes were really puffy. I began to think the worse.

Was she sick?

Did something happen to her family?

My thoughts were racing. My heart was aching. I didn't even know what was wrong with her, but the very fact that she was hurting made me hurt inside.

"Erin. What's wrong? Please tell me."

Erin looked up from where she was leaning against the locker, stared me in my eyes, and said, "I'm pregnant."

I pulled Erin toward my chest and held her for like three minutes. "Oh, Erin. I'm so sorry! Ohhh," I cried.

"I'm so sorry Erin. We will get through this together. It's going to be alright. Ok? It's going to be alright Erin. I'm here."

I held her again and then we realized the hallways had gotten quiet. The bells had rung, and we were late to class. I didn't care. My friend was hurting and she needed me. I walked Erin to her class and then went to my Spanish class, tardy.

3

COLLEGE, WORK, AND A STROKE

Senior year had arrived. Already! The sounds of 12th graders screaming down the hall, throwing streamers, jumping up and down and chanting our senior theme! Wow! Didn't I just get here? Wasn't I just having freshman jitters my ninth-grade year? Was I really finished hearing Mrs. Talbert screech when she talks? Was I finally almost free from feeling Mr. Baker's spit on my forehead when he talked? And dang— Was this the end of seeing Mrs. Pittman's wig on sideways? And was I finally able to walk away from Ms. Truman, the *bougie* teacher whose class I failed miserably and asked for makeup work? I remember that bougie teacher agreed to let me stay after school to make up my "F" in her class.

"I'm here for my make-up assignment Ms. Truman."

"Ok, here you go," as she hands me the duster, broom, and dustpan.

"What's this for Ms. Truman?"

"That's for you to sweep my floor and dust my desk and cabinets."

"Ummm…."

"And when you're done with that, clean out my desk drawers and wipe down my cabinets."

I took that broom and wacked her upside her head.

Ok. That was just my imagination! I opened my eyes after imagining that scene in my head and smiled really big at her and said, "Yes ma'am, Ms. Truman."

Over one hour later, Ms. Truman looked at me and said, "Ok, your grade has been changed to a D."

I was looking for an apartment to move into immediately after I graduated high school. College had not crossed my mind. I had it settled in my mind, "I'm not about to waste my time!" Then, here comes my mother in my ear.

"Tichina, what colleges are you looking at? Have you applied for any?"

"No ma'am. I'm not going to college."

"What? Girl! Tuh!"

Her favorite phrase when she wanted to be sarcastic was always *Tuh* as in *You're so funny that I forgot to laugh!*

"What Mama? I'm not going to college."
"Tuh!"

"My friend and I are going to get an apartment mama and I'm gonna get a job."

I could see my mother's sarcastic face turn into a serious face. "China, you don't want to be stuck on those little bitty jobs all your life barely having a paycheck after paying bills. You need something to sustain you. You have a chance to go to college, so you need to go.

"But mama."

"But nothing. You're going to college. Now which one do you want to go to?

So, that was it. I was going to college. My little pipe dream of getting an apartment and a job was out and the University of Arkansas at Little Rock was in. I was not very excited about college; nevertheless, I went. And I found out—*shhhh...* I found out that (*come a little closer to the page*)...I found out that I...I really loved college!

It was absolutely amazing! It was totally different from high school. Ugh. High school. I was so ready to get out of that place! But college...

college was different. It was another atmosphere! It was where I felt I belonged. It was my community. A town within its own. My new home! And because I'm the baby, it gave me the illusion that I was really far way; however, I knew I could always get inside of my little gray 2002 Ford Escort and drive ten minutes to my mother's house.

On the very first day of college, I was anxious! I raised my hand all cheerfully in class because I had to go to the restroom! I couldn't hold it anymore! The professor looked at me, "Yes, do you have a question?"

"Yes. May I go to the restroom?"

"Umm. You're in college now, ma'am. You don't have to raise your hand to go to the restroom."

"Ohhh…excuse me," I whispered as I lifted my index finger up to walk through the aisles past students to get to the restroom. *Great Tichina! Now, you're acting like you're in church about to sneak out at offering time!* As if those were not enough first day freshmen bloopers, I walked to my class waiting on the bell to ring. Now, how was I supposed to know when I was tardy or about to be tardy? Gheesh! This college stuff was wearing me out! But I got the hang of it! And I loved it! Oh, the independence; the freedom; the people I met; the dorms; the activities; the events! Ahhh, college was it! I was here for it all!

College brought out the worst of me, but then it brought out the *best* of me! Like many freshmen teenage college students, I was swept into the infamous party life. *Sigh*. I had fun. Lots of fun. Then I could hear my mother, brother, and sister in my ear about saving partying until after college, so I slacked down on doing that so much to get into my studies. I started excelling in my studies and got the hang of managing my life. It was time to get a job! I got hired on at The Sandwich Hut and loved it! I worked at The Sandwich Hut for a long while; then, I got hired on at Wally Universe and loved it even more! It was my "at college" dream job. Everyone there was awesome, and I loved working the cash register. I was making good money for only being a college student with absolutely no bills except a phone bill and some gas to get from point A to B. I was living the life! I was so grateful and was on my way to obtaining my bachelor's degree. I couldn't have imagined life would be so great.

Then, my life changed forever.

It had only been three months that I had been working at Wally Universe. I found myself with a headache, the most excruciating pain I'd ever felt in my entire life one day while at my sister's house. I tried to eat and couldn't. The next thing I know, I was on the bathroom floor at my sister's house and had fallen. I couldn't get up. I couldn't walk. I couldn't talk and I was at the house alone.

"Tichina?"

I heard my brother in law knocking on the bathroom door. Apparently, he had just returned to the house and was checking on the loud thump he'd heard.

"Tichina! Are you okay?"

I can't talk. I can't walk. Lord, what's going on?

"Tichina! Are you okay?"

Lord, let me just be able to answer him. I know the words I want to say, but they aren't coming out of my mouth. I can't make it to the door.

"Tichina! What's wrong? Can you hear me?"

I can hear you Rell. I can hear you. Something is wrong.

I am certain my brother in law was frantic by this time being that I was not responding and he had heard the loud thump from when I had fallen. So, the next thing I heard was…

"Tichina, you have 5 seconds to answer me or I'm knocking this bathroom door down. Tichina! Can you hear me? Answer me!"

I hear you Rell. I can't answer you. Something is wrong.

My brother in law knocked the bathroom door in and helped me up. He called my sister and my mom, and I was rushed to the hospital. I don't remember much, but I do remember lying in that hospital bed unable to talk and unable to move part of my body.

4

30 DAYS
OF HOSPITALIZATION

Say it with me: *Arterial Ischemic Stroke.*
19-Year-Old African American Female.

No previous illness or diseases.

Arterial Ischemic Stroke.

19-Year-Old African American College student majoring in Social Work with a 'B' grade point average.

Active in campus programs and a part-time employee at Wally Universe.

Vibrant, full of life, and motivated about education.

No previous medical problems. No previous illnesses.

Arterial Ischemic Stroke.

On June 11, 2012, only one year after I had graduated high school, and one year of being in college, I laid in the hospital bed day after day, unable to walk or talk. I'd had a brain injury; perhaps one of the most advanced brain injuries ever.

I was drugged on medication. I was in and out of consciousness. My entire family came to see me. I still have bears today from when they visited me and provided gifts for me to cheer me up. I had a great support system. That meant a lot to me. My mother was doing some serious praying! I vividly remember Mama praying. When I woke up, Mama was praying. When company came and when they left, Mama was praying. She called up prayer circles and prayer warriors.

While everyone came to visit me, I could only muster a smile. I couldn't talk back; I couldn't communicate with them or respond, so I just smiled. Several pastors came to see me. My pastor, Apostle Kingsley, and my church family came to see me. They prayed for me and helped to comfort me.

I remember being in a smaller hospital and they had me sitting there for days. There was a social worker who actually diagnosed me before the doctor did. Well, not officially; but she said,

"This sounds like a stroke." My sisters and mom said the same thing. Those doctors didn't listen, so Mama transferred me to another hospital. When I was sitting in that hospital, there was a woman who kept telling Mama that I have to keep moving my hand. I couldn't walk. I couldn't talk.

It wasn't until I made it to the new hospital that I was properly diagnosed with the ischemic stroke. The doctors did not have a good prognosis for me. They told my mom that I may regain some of my physical abilities back and some of my speech, but nothing was certain. They said I may not be able to drive again or return to school, let alone get my college degree.

I was still mute and couldn't verbalize my pain. So, the pain was trapped inside and all I could do was cry from within.

By this time, I had been in the hospital for two weeks. It was two weeks' worth of running tests, trying to discover where the stroke could have come from, and trying to figure out a plan for me to get well. Meanwhile, I was thinking about how I was supposed to be returning to college in two months. I was worried about my job at Wally Universe because I loved that job so much. I had planned to work there my entire college career. It was my "college" dream job.

Dear Lord, can I just get up and walk and return back to my life?
Can you open my mouth and allow me to speak?
Is this real?
Why are all of these doctors gathered around in a huddle so much every day?
Am I going to make it out of this?

My doctors scheduled physical therapy and speech therapy for me at the hospital. It was around the clock therapy for me. That was the hardest thing I've ever had to do, but not one time did I want to quit. Not one time did I think of giving up.

I wanted my life back.

I wanted to return to college.

I was only 19 years old. Life had just begun for me and it had been going well.

So, before I could even talk again, I was working on regaining my leg strength and my ability to walk. The physical therapists worked with my hands and feet and told me to make a habit of doing it with and without them. At first, I thought, "How am I going to do this without you all? I mean, I tell my brain to move my leg, but it won't move. I tell my brain to move my hand, but it won't move."

While I was in speech therapy, I began to make sounds. I just wanted to talk normal again. I just wanted to walk again. Until I could make words, the nurses directed my family and me to write on a board to communicate with them. But here's the thing: I had absolutely no movement in my right hand which is the hand I wrote with. My left hand had a little movement by now and that's the hand I used. Remember that story of how I was ambidextrous? Well, that ability to write with my left and right hand came in handy! See! That's the kind of God we serve. I was learning to count my blessings.

I mean, don't get me wrong; my handwriting was awful, like worse than a kindergartener, but I was writing and communicating through writing with my left hand. So, I thanked God.

I left the hospital in a wheelchair after 30 days of hospitalization. I began to improve. I went from a wheelchair to a cane and from a cane to only a brace in my shoe. I know it was nobody but God to explain how I survived and to explain my improvements the way I had.

According to strokecenter.org, stroke is the third leading cause of death and more than

140,000 people die each year from stroke in the United States. "Strokes can and do occur at *any* age. On average, someone in the United States has a stroke every 40 seconds." [1]

So, what is an arterial ischemic stroke?

"This type of stroke is caused by a blockage in an artery that supplies blood to the brain. The blockage reduces the blood flow and oxygen to the brain, leading to damage or death of brain cells. If circulation isn't restored quickly, brain damage can be permanent." [2]

I sat in the first hospital for days with no treatment before being transported to the other hospital. Being that time is of the most important essence with a stroke and the fact that the first hospital did not respond within the appropriate amount of time, I should not have been able to recover, according to medical research.

According to webmd.com, "If a stroke is not caught and treated early, permanent brain damage or death can result." [3] So, to be able to progress from a wheelchair to a walking cane to only a brace in a matter of months was a miracle; yet another badge added to God's line of miracles for my life.

5

FURY, FRUSTRATION AND RAGE

A person goes through so many highs and lows during a sickness or any life-changing event such as a stroke. There are days you want to emotionally stay up and try your best, but it feels nearly impossible. Listen, the stroke had interrupted my *entire* life. Wally Universe held my position, but not for long. I was excited when my sister took all the paperwork there and they agreed to hold my position. I had hope, you know; hope that I'd recuperate fully; hope that I'd be able to speak again, think right again, and walk right again. But that didn't happen. I struggled so much for so long. After a couple of months, Wally Universe stopped holding my position and I was officially let go. That broke me in so many ways. How did I turn from being a successful working college student to a handicapped, unemployed non-college student? By the way, that's the only time you'll ever hear me say the word handicapped when referring to myself. I hate it. **I hate that word. I'm not handicapped. I'm independent.**

I suffered memory loss since the day I had the stroke. At first, I was not able to remember words. It was difficult for me to recall the right things.

For example, when speaking to someone and my intention is to say couch, I might say apple. I'd say something that is totally unrelated to the item I'm thinking of. It's so frustrating! It made me feel so stupid around others. I felt so small.

I couldn't say certain words and couldn't construct the smallest bit of sentences properly. On top of all of that, I began to lose my hair. I was on all kinds of medications such as blood thinners and the like; medication I was told I'll have to take the rest of my life to avoid another stroke. These medications made my hair fall out. I was not only suffering physically, but now emotionally and psychologically due to my appearance and my walk. When people look at me, they stare. They all treated me like I was helpless and couldn't do for myself. It's ironic how life plays itself out. Remember, I always had some sort of inclination toward people with handicaps when I was young. I always felt so sorry for them and wished better for them and secretly, I'd say, "I pray that never happens to me." And then it happened. I had become the people I prayed not to. Most people would blame God. No, I didn't blame God. I knew he had rescued me from the hand of the enemy that tried to kill me. But I did get mad. Oh, I got angry and depressed and more....

By this time, I had been out of college for one and a half years. Because of this, I lost my scholarship! Lord, help. Everything was being ripped away from me. My job, my schooling, my financial security and more.

I was approved to only take one college class due to my physical and mental impairments. And it could only be like an arts course or something simple. I wanted to do this college thing *so badly*. So, I took the one class: Art Appreciation. But even that was too hard. I couldn't process it. My mind couldn't process it or keep up with any of it. I cried so hard. I was so frustrated. No one understood what I was dealing with inside.

When people said things to me, I could barely

remember. They had to tell me things over and over again. In order for me to grasp something, it had to be exact or it would confuse and frustrate me. For example, if someone said they'd be there to pick me up at 3:00, I'd stare at the clock and if they came at 3:01, it aggravated me. I felt like I was wrong. Time was one of the few things I got right. I couldn't get words right or my memory right, but I got time right. Therefore, it was like it kind of offset my brain or set off negative brainwaves and I couldn't handle it.

I was gifted. I had talent. I could write poetry and recite it like Maya Angelou's protégé. But now, I could hardly speak anything more than a toddler's babble.

I had to relearn my alphabet, relearn how to count, relearn how to spell, and relearn how to talk. I spoke like a kindergartener and processed information like a foreigner who was new to the country.

Some people say there are more good days than bad. But I experienced more sad days, more bad days, and more painful days than ever. There were so many sorrows and losses that stemmed from the ischemic stroke. I was the girl who could walk on the tips of her toes like a professional ballerina. I was the girl they were signing up for track in their heads. I was fast on my feet. Now, I didn't even have the capability of running if I tried. By this time, I was mad at my brain. Mad because I told it to do something and it wouldn't. It refused. My brain didn't work the same. My brain didn't work like everyone else's anymore. What did I do to deserve this? It's frustrating because I knew what I wanted to say, and I said it in my head, but it didn't come out the way I thought it in my head. It didn't come out the way I told my brain to. People held a conversation with me and I tried to respond and communicate with them, and it took me so long to get out what I was trying to say. So, they got impatient and began trying to finish my sentences and thoughts for me.

I wanted to yell, *"No! That's not what I'm trying to say!"* So, I became angry. Angry at being unable to run again. Angry at being unable to stand on my toes again. Angry because of that special talent that I never knew was a talent, and the fact that I couldn't do it anymore! Funny how we don't take the time to value things when we should.

I was gifted. I had talent. I could write poetry and recite it like Maya Angelou's protégé. But now, I could hardly speak anything more than a toddler's babble. I felt stupid. I felt dumb. I felt incapable and stuck in somebody else's body. How did I go from being capable to incapable? Able to unable?

I've always been a fashionista! I've always been that girly girl who loves makeup, fashion, and a fresh hairdo! Now, I only had one arm and was unable to do my hair, which is one of the things I really wanted to do.

I was now unable to wear heels. I had to wear a particular kind of shoe; a particular kind of outfit. I can't even tie my own shoes. I have to put the shoe strings inside of the shoe. In order to wear my brace on my leg and foot, there was a special kind of shoe I was required to wear. These shoes were gaudy and all kinds of ugly. I felt ugly. I didn't feel pretty anymore. The sadness overwhelmed me. I tried to be positive and I was, but the everyday adjustments and inability to do anything for myself, and the frustration with my brain and my words all became too much for me.

My mom was there day in and day out taking care of me. She had to do everything for me. She had to help me to the bathroom, do my hair, help me eat, wipe my mouth, and everything under the sun. I've always liked to have my own individuality and independence, but this stroke had robbed me of even that small luxury. When I ate, there was food all over my mouth which I couldn't feel because of the numbness of my jaw.

Today, there are no issues with feeding myself, wiping my mouth, or going to the bathroom. That was all temporary and I'm glad that stage is over! However, I'm still partially paralyzed in my right hand and right foot. My ankles and toes won't move, and fingers won't move on the right side. I have a drooping arm.

As the years went on, and I progressed deeper into my 20's, I became very sad and depressed thinking men will never notice me. That breaks my heart, even unto today. When men see me, the first thing I say is, "I had a stroke." The stroke greatly impacted my self-concept and self-esteem.

I'm in my later twenties now and it breaks my heart, you know, to feel like men don't actually want me for me. Men approach me often, but it's hard to think that I'm actually *wanted* by men. I think to myself, "Nobody wants me." I feel like they will see my limp and the way I walk, and I think myself into believing they don't actually want me even though they do. One guy even said to me, "You're pretty and if anybody ever talks about you having a stroke, they are not worth it anyway." That was so sweet, I know, but in my mind, I don't think that's true. It's hard because I'm approached by men telling me I'm beautiful and wanted, but I still feel unattractive because of my walk, because of how I talk, because of this thing they see as a disability. I feel so unpretty at times. So, unworthy.

And as far as a career?

I think, "What job is going to ever hire me?"

I think, *"No job will want a disabled person like me." Some may laugh at me and wonder what in the world made me ever come to an interview. Some will show pity and still give me an interview but will trash my resume before I can ever get to the parking lot. Nobody wants me. Not a man. Not a friend. Not even a job. I won't ever be the social worker I've dreamed of my entire life."*

Although not exactly reality, but these were all my thoughts, day in and day out.

So how do I compensate for this? How do I cope with all of this?

I started drinking. Not just a glass or two and not just wine. Hardcore drinking. It was my medicine. It was my boyfriend that wanted me. It was the guy who noticed me. It was the beauty that I could no longer see in me; the joy I hadn't felt in two years. It was the peace away from the half brain that couldn't get anything right; couldn't remember anything; couldn't process things accurately. I had a date night almost every night with Rum and coke and Long Island Iced Tea. But Tequila was my best friend. Because by this time, I didn't have any friends anymore. Most of them just stopped calling me. And the others, I pushed away because of the disability.

I didn't want any phone calls from anybody! I didn't want any visits. I was so afraid of how I looked even to go outside.

I was embarrassed about my arm and leg.

On top of all of this, I had lost *so much weight* that my collar bone was showing; it was sticking out. I looked so frail. I felt miserable.

And to add misery to my being miserable, people would say, "Ohh, girl you've lost so much weight! You're so skinny! Girl, you need some meat on those bones. Girl, you need to eat."

Oh, the insensitivity from people and their ignorance. They spoke as if I wanted this; like I had chosen this. I didn't want to go anywhere or talk to anyone. **I was depressed for two years.** Sadly, "Post-Stroke Depression" is a real thing.

According to stroke.org, "[Post-Stroke] Depression is a common experience for stroke survivors. It's often caused by biochemical changes in the brain. When the brain is injured, the survivor may not be able to feel positive emotions. Depression can also be a normal psychological reaction to the losses from stroke. Here are some of the common symptoms of depression:

- Persistent sad, anxious or "empty" mood
- Restlessness and irritability
- Feelings of hopelessness, pessimism, guilt, worthlessness or helplessness
- Loss of interest or pleasure in hobbies and activities, including sex
- Decreased energy and fatigue, and feeling "slowed down"
- Difficulty concentrating, remembering and making decisions
- Insomnia, early-morning awakening or oversleeping
- Appetite and/or weight changes
- Thoughts of death or suicide, or suicide attempts

Depression may make the rehabilitation process more challenging for survivors to do the hard work required." [1]

My nickname is Miracle, but by this time, **I felt like my name was Misery instead of Miracle and there had been some kind of mistake in my name.** I thought that by my attending church that it would magically reappear. I thought I'd regain my feelings back in my hands and feet. That was the goal. I was furious! This time when I got mad, I blamed it on God. I began saying He wasn't healing me. I started listening to rap music because I was angry at Him. I was angry at God, so I called myself retaliating; acting out.

I talked like a kindergartner or more specifically; a preschooler. See, I didn't realize how these things can take time.

"God hadn't forgotten about me," I thought.

He would soon show me that He hadn't forgotten about me, because as you will see later, God gave my voice and speech back little by little and then much by much.

But at the time, I thought, "Why me? Why did this happen to me?"

I was mixing up words. My family couldn't understand what I said. I felt embarrassed around them when I talked and when I walked, so I pushed them away. And the others just stopped being my friends. I didn't have any friends. I didn't have a boyfriend. I couldn't do for myself.

And why is it that I could feel numb in my damn hand and foot, but not in my heart?

Why were my other body parts paralyzed, but not my heart?

That's what I needed to be paralyzed! I needed my heart to be numb.

I know God wasn't pleased with my use of curse words. That stroke had gotten the best of me, tried turning me into someone I wasn't. I was broken. Heartbroken. And so, I drank it away. I drank until my heart became as paralyzed as my hand and foot. Now! Take that, stroke! Forget you and forget where you came from!

That Ischemic stroke caused me to be mad, hysterical, and violent! Or maybe it was the alcohol that caused it; but it all stemmed from that dang ischemic stroke!

Ugh! *Insert curse word here.*

And another expletive. Because I was enraged! Furious!

I had been positive and uplifting for 2 years. I had praised God, loved God, smiled around people, apologized to those I may have hurt in the past, and more. I was thankful for my progress, but I was still here.

So many people said, "Oh, Tichina, you're doing so marvelous after your stroke." But I didn't see what they saw in me.

I looked at my fingers and they didn't work. So, I was angry! What were they talking about? I looked at my toes and my toes didn't

I drank until my heart became as paralyzed as my hand and foot.

move! So, what are they talking about? I was so mad! So sad. I looked at my right leg and my right leg couldn't bend, *still*. I checked in with my brain and it was still mixing up words, calling a pencil an apple and a chair a kite and making me repeat the last sentence I heard when trying to respond to someone. The words I spoke were still irrelevant to the conversation at hand. A conversation with someone about how my day had been prompted me to respond about the ketchup I'd just put on my French fries. What was wrong with me? What was wrong with my freaking brain?!

I grew so angry that I even stopped exercising my hand when I knew that's what I was supposed to do. I stopped even for a year because I was so mad. I had to have a driver everywhere I went. My mother drove me around everywhere. I couldn't drive, and the doctors said I would never be able to.

Drinking put me in a happy place. I went from being depressed to happy when I drank. Soon, I started hanging with a new group of "friends". These "friends" and I bought liquor, got drunk, and spent the night at hotel rooms. We drank, slept around at hotels, and got turned up with men.

"Those people are a bad influence, China," cried my mom. "They're nothing but trouble China. You don't need to hang around them."

I didn't care. At least somebody wanted to hang out with me. I just wanted to feel normal again. I wanted to be *wanted* again by friends who wanted to hang with me. I wanted friends to call me up again just to ask to hang out. I wanted friends. That stroke put me in a really low place. People didn't understand.

I just *needed*.

Needed what? I needed to feel a sense of belonging.

After two years of being a stroke victim, limping everywhere I go, unable to walk straight, unable to talk correctly, unable to dress myself, unable to wear my hair the way I used to, I felt I didn't belong anywhere anymore. There was no acceptance anywhere anymore, or at least that's what I felt. So, along with the other "friends", I bought supplies so that we could all smoke, drink alcohol, and do lots of unproductive things.

But I was *cool* again. I was *wanted* again.

I was able to laugh with people my age again. I felt accepted even if it was phony; I was able to fool myself into believing this was acceptance. And it's what I needed at the time. Or at least I thought so. But as you can probably guess, that all ended badly. The girls I hung out with ended up disrespecting my mom very badly. My sisters couldn't understand why I hung out with those people. If I could only tell them: *"I've been depressed for almost two years; sometimes not seeing a reason to live. I'm very lonely and feel like the little kid at school no one wants to play with. I'm depressed and feel dead, so this fake love and fake acceptance is the only thing making me feel alive."*

6

30 Minutes to Cry

Drinking had become my therapy. Looking at myself in the mirror seeing the frail body that I was, the depression grew worse. The devil started attacking my mind. My brain already didn't work the way it used to; now he was playing with my mind: telling me things that weren't true, trying to get me to end my life. He's the father of lies! He tried to turn me against God; the one who had kept me! I was still angry at God; angry at those who loved me; angry at everyone around me. That was, until I got drunk. I thought, "Lord, I go to church faithfully. This is going to fix my leg. It's going to magically happen that my hand will work again. My shoulder that slants down will be straightened. I will be able to talk normal again, but when that didn't happen after a couple of years, I became angry.

I didn't want to live anymore. I cried all the time. My life was a bigger mess emotionally than it was physically. My external wasn't the only handicap; now my emotions were; my heart was; and my mind was. I couldn't do for myself. I couldn't drive. I couldn't walk right. I couldn't talk properly. How did my life go from being normal to *this* unfortunate abnormality in the blink of an eye? I cried day in and day out. Everything literally reminded me of my "normal" days. *Sigh.*

And when I rode in the car with my mom from destination to destination, I remembered how my brain worked properly to communicate to my leg to command it to move and walk to the car and how my brain worked effortlessly to communicate to my now paralyzed hand to turn the steering wheel. Oh, what I would have given at this point in my life to drive again.

My mom is my world. I give so much thanks and appreciation to her for the sacrifices she didn't have to do, but she did anyway as a result of my stroke. In between her jobs, she drove me everywhere: to doctor's appointments, and more. So, I'm grateful for that. Beyond grateful. But it made me think of how I wish I could drive at that time.

So, I cried. Everything made me cry. I cried all the time. Then one day, a counselor's words changed my life. I went to a therapist because I wanted to know how to get over it. It had been *years* and I was still crying and depressed and I wanted it to end. The coun-

My external wasn't the only handicap; now my emotions were; my heart was; and my mind was.

selor told me a story about a lady with a burned face. This lady must walk around all her life with her face being altered with major burns. She told me how it weighed on the lady's confidence and self-esteem. The counselor explained the traumatic affects that the facial deformity had on the women's inner being. I could definitely relate. It's like people stare at her all day wondering what happened to her and wanting to give her pity the way they do me. I hate that.

I hate the pity they have in their eyes when they see me.

I hate the way they act like I'm incapable of anything because of my inadequacies.

I hate being the stares of little kids and adults. I fear the kids will point and ask "Mommy, what's wrong with her?" However, the next thing the counselor said helped to change my entire out-look on coping with this stroke thing. She said the lady with the burned face gives herself five minutes to cry and then she goes on with her day. The counselor said, "You may not ever get over it, but that's a way of not letting it overtake you." That made a light bulb go off. I get it! Give yourself a limit! It's okay to cry, but it's not okay to stay there.

So, I give myself 30 minutes to cry. I'm not quite at the five minutes yet, but I've made great progress. I get really depressed sometimes, even still. But that's not going to stop me though. I'm still going to have a happy life. If I find myself crying for longer than 30 minutes, I call Mama! And so, the crying stops and I get to go on with my life. After all, I am a miracle! My life has proved it over and over again. The 30-minute crying helped me to see a few things:

It helped me understand what others saw when they continued to say, "Oh, China, you're doing so marvelous after your stroke." I was able to focus on the miracle in it all instead of the struggles from it. The miracle is that I lived. The miracle is that although I was limping, I was walking. I was not bedridden anymore. I was not confined to a wheelchair anymore. My speech had improved to a point to where I didn't have to write on paper as my means of communication. Now, I could have a conversation with others. My speech is no longer like a kindergartener's babble. The list goes on.

It helped me to focus on the blessings I had within my family. I thought about where I would be if I didn't have them here helping me through this all. At least I have someone to help me since I'm unable to do my hair. I have a mother who would otherwise be in the bed, but instead comes and takes the hairbrush to brush and style my hair. Since I was unable to drive, I have a mother who chauffeured me around even in the middle of her busy work day. While my sister is the busiest person I know, she came and helped me with my homework and schoolwork from time to time when I struggled with it. And another sister who selflessly talks to me on the phone all night, drives an hour away to spend time with me, and does so much more for me. I have a brother who writes encouraging words to me and another brother who visits me. So, while I take 30 minutes to cry about my very unfortunate struggles from this stroke, the rest of the 23.5 hours in the day belong to focusing on blessings! Isn't God a good God?

It helped me understand that my life is far from over! When the enemy told me that my life was over, and I believed him, I now understand that couldn't be farther from the truth. I started back school eventually and began taking classes which is beyond a miracle. That signified promise and a future!

So, I'm grateful for that counselor because 30 minutes to cry is my new philosophy! I may cry, but I will get up! I will wipe my tears, and I will run on, with or without the ability to use my right hand and right foot. Yes, even if it takes 30 minutes to cry.

7

WHY AM I STILL HERE?

What was I still doing here? Really, why was I still alive? How did I survive a stroke that a hospital didn't even properly respond to in time? How did I regain my ability to talk again? How did I progress from that wheelchair to that cane to the ankle brace to no walking equipment at all? Why did I survive as the one year old who was hit by the back of my aunt's car as she put it in reverse? Why did I survive all the car accidents and those where I fell out of the car onto a high trafficked highway? All I know is I asked God to let me live for some kind of purpose and He did. I'm trying to figure out what it is. I haven't found it yet, but I guarantee you I won't stop until I do. I started evangelizing on the church street team ministry with my mom. I was really scared, but sometimes, you have to make sacrifices for God. I just wanted to give back. God had been so good to me and I found out that I find joy in spreading the word about God. I began telling people everywhere I went of how God healed me and how Jesus saves. Street Team ministry is *something* though. It's not for the weak *(laughing out loud)*. We often go into the rough neighborhoods and spread the good news. Some people are receptive, and some aren't. I also pray a lot for people. God places people on my spirit and I am led by God to pray for them. I do it frequently. My mother said when I was just a little girl that one day I would be a prayer warrior. Hmm.

I like to pray for others. I know God hears my prayers because he places them on my spirit just so that I can pray for them. So, I say to myself, "I wouldn't have been able to do this if I weren't alive to see this day."

I know God has more for me to do. I don't know exactly what that is yet. My pastor prophesied that I was going to be a praise dancer. He didn't even know that I used to be a praise dancer back in the day. I would love to praise dance again one day. God has said I'm going to be able to walk straight again one day. And guess what?

I believe in miracles. I am one. In fact, I'm a

ball of miracles. A walking miracle. God doesn't perform miracles to watch them die. He performs miracles for his glory; so that his miracles can live; so that we can go testify of his goodness and his wonderful works.

~⟡

So, after a while, I was blessed to begin taking more classes a semester. The doctors had previously said that I should only be able to take basic classes such as art and music because my brain wouldn't be able to accommodate the rigor of the higher-level classes. Basically, it was diagnosed and prescribed that I could take classes just for leisure; but I'd never be able to take the classes that a college degree would require. However, the God of miracles that I serve; you know... the one who made my brain? Well, He made a way that my brain began to gradually grasp the material and I was soon taking 9 hours! I went from 3 hours to 9 hours per semester. This was not quite a full-time college student though and so I ended up with no choice but to lose my scholarship. They told me they could only put it on hold for so long. They held my scholarship for only a year and since my brain hadn't caught up that quickly, I lost it. No mercy from them at all. My scholarship required me to be a full-time student and since I wasn't, I was left with no financial aid.

Bummer.

But I was determined. I decided to pay for my schooling out of pocket. I wanted that degree. I deserved it. A major arterial ischemic stroke came and tried to claim my life. I wasn't going to let it win. I wasn't going to let it take another thing from me. I wasn't going to allow the stroke to disable me. Regardless of how the world viewed me, I would not be some stroke's handicap! It was then that it dawned on me: I was left here for some higher purpose.

One reason is to show the world that if I can graduate college, God can help them do the same. If I can overcome the challenges I have endured with the help of God, so can they. See, my physical limitations taught me that God is still God and that He can be seen even within the challenges we face.

He is in the air that I breathe when I wake up because the stroke did not leave me dependent on an oxygen mask.

He is in the awareness of my surroundings be-cause the stroke didn't turn me into a vegetable, being unaware that I was even in the world.

See, I learned that God takes delight in my

progress and many of my prayers have already been answered.

So, I was taking courses and paying for them with all the income I received per month. And I was struggling, educationally. I had to work harder than I ever had in my entire life. My brain couldn't quite process the information in the timeframe that the work required. Even with my tutoring, I was still struggling to catch on and keep up. My sister helped a lot when she could. But she has several companies, kids,

Regardless of how the world viewed me, I would not be some stroke's handicap!

and a husband, so I didn't feel comfortable calling on her all the time. The disability department at the university mandated the professors to give me more time to complete my assignments. The problem with that is some professors complied; some didn't.

Trying to explain my limitations to my professors was like trying to speak Spanish to an American who only speaks English. They couldn't speak my language; let alone understand it.

They could see my physical disability on the outside: the limp in my walk, the disproportion of my shoulder, the crippled hand; but they couldn't see the left side of my brain that was no longer communicating effectively to the words in their textbooks.

They couldn't see how I read the same thing over and over and forgot what I had just read due to the death of some of the cells in my brain.

They couldn't see that by the time they got to the 50th minute of the class instruction, that my brain was still trying to process what was taught during the 15th minute of the class instruction.

Or did they just not care?

Did they not care that the instructions they gave the class should have been modified to a level that I could grasp? Did they not care that the part of my brain that allowed me to effectively ask the right questions in class had been blocked which prevented my ability to get answers like other students?

My brain had been *attacked!*

That's another word for a stroke: a brain attack. It's like a heart attack, but on the brain. My brain had been *attacked!* Aggressively.

I reported the professors, but nothing happened. So, even with tutors and the extra assistance from the disability department, I was pretty much on my own.

Until, I realized I wasn't. I had God. I had my

faith in Him.

Although that faith had been deeply and tremendously tested, it was there. My mother had instilled it in me and I had not strayed from it. So, I prayed. I received F's; I often had to drop required classes and lose money, only to be required to take them again later. But I didn't give up. I prayed even harder and worked even harder. I had to work at least 4 or 5 times harder than the average college student. I was at the school before my classes started and was there hours after they ended.

That's right. So many nights, I was at the school from 7:30 a.m. to 11:30 p.m. I had to succeed. Maybe others would think it's not fair for them to have to be required to do all of this just to pass a couple of courses. But I didn't think it was unfair. I thought it was an opportunity that God have given me to show forth His glory. Every single person on earth has challenges. Who am I to pick mine? If it wasn't this but was some other challenge I had to face, I wouldn't like that one either.

I knew now that I was blessed and that it wasn't the end of the world for me. I cried though. I cried a lot. So many times, I had worked on one little project for *days* and weeks that would have taken another person less than two hours. I got frustrated, cried, quit, cried, and then started on it again. This process was repeated for just about every single assignment. But I kept on witnessing by myself about God to others that I saw on the street and also while working on the street team ministry at my church. And I kept on praying to God. And I kept on fighting and working.

School was my breakfast, lunch, and dinner. I didn't have a choice.

And soon, I began making A's and B's!

Wow! Did you hear that?

Winner! Winner!

Yes, the stroke survivor (whose professors weren't the nicest or the least bit of lenient on her) was now making A's and B's. One professor literally told me to suck it up. I was so angry and hurt. He told me I should not get special privileges and he wouldn't give them to me. I couldn't let that stop me. All I could see was that degree and one day working as a social worker for kids. I love kids so much!

My sister told me I was an inspiration to others. I always look at her as being inspiring with all that she has accomplished and all that she does for others, but to hear that from her made me go, "What? Huh? Really?" She called me heroic because in her words, she says I don't give up, I don't complain, I don't throw myself a pity party, I don't use the stroke as an excuse, I still praise God and serve God, and I am still as independent as my Grandma Vernell.

Ha! That last part made me laugh. Let me explain Granny Vernell to you! She was 95 years old and was still cooking for herself and cleaning for herself. Granny Vernell wouldn't let another person pick up a broom and sweep her floors! It wasn't pride. It was independence. She was a do it yourself as long as you have breath kind of woman! Well, I won't say my sister is right about Granny Vernell and me, but I'll admit that whatever I can do with one arm, I do, and I won't let any family member do it for me. I can remember when I was first able to wear tennis shoes again. This same sister tried to tie my shoes for me.

"Aht. Aht. I got this", I snapped.

Whoa! Ok. I'm stepping back Frick and Frat!" exclaimed my sister.

I don't know what that phrase meant and I'm sure neither does she! But she was referring to me as being my granny and myself in one. It took me about 5 minutes, but I finally managed to tie that shoe. And she waited and watched and allowed me to do it. If I have the ability, I like to do it. **I don't allow the "disability" to disable me or the "handicap" to handicap me, you know?** I like to overcome what is trying to overcome me. I don't like to use limitations as an excuse. They will not limit me!

Does that make me inspirational? Does that mean I'm an inspiration? I didn't see myself as heroic or inspirational. But I'm still here and I've been wondering why on earth am I still here from a stroke that was supposed to leave me 100% immobile or dead. If God left me to be an inspiration to even one person, that makes my life worth living and it makes living through the challenges worth it. I know this isn't all. I know there's more to my life's meaning.

And I am getting closer to understanding why I'm here as the days go on. So, I'm choosing to hold on!

I still believe I'll walk straight one day.

I still believe I'll talk with 100% accuracy again one day.

I still believe that my memory and processing will return with all efficacy one day. I can see myself praise dancing again like my pastor prophesied. I believe one day, I'll just praise my way into full deliverance! You know why? Because I'm still here for a reason. God left me here for a reason!

8

I am Not My Stroke

I had made it to my senior year in college! I was majoring in Sociology and minoring in Non-profit Management. I began my internship at a non-profit organization and finished with flying colors. I would now be earning my CNP: Certain Non-profit Professional certificate! This certificate is the only *national* nonprofit credential that prepares graduates for leadership in the nonprofit sector. I was so excited! The hours of studying got even longer and harder. I was practically living in the school library when I wasn't in class. My mom would call and say, "China, are you ready for me to pick you up yet?"

I'd reply, "Another hour Mama."

At ten o' clock: "China, are you ready now?"

"No ma'am. Another hour."

At Midnight: "I'm ready Mama."

This was almost every day. I'd get there before 8:00 a.m. and stay until midnight. I literally closed the campus library down.

In the beginning of 2019, the specialists went inside of my car and converted the break pad to the far left side and put a left foot pedal in and removed the "normal" right foot gas pedal so that I could drive with my left foot. I took lessons by professionals who were trained in modifying vehicles with adaptive equipment for those with disabilities. They also put a device on my steering wheel so that I could steer the vehicle with my left hand smoothly since it would be impossible to do with my left hand on the original steering wheel.

And what do you know? This young lady who was never supposed to drive is now driving! Moreover, this young lady who was scared out of her mind to ever drive again is now driving! It had been seven entire years since I'd driven a car; seven entire years since I had the stroke. Seven entire years since the doctors said I would never drive again. And now I was driving!

I used to be so afraid to live alone. What would happen if I fell and there was no one there to help me up? What if I was cooking and something happened to me while cooking? What if someone broke into my apartment and I know I wouldn't be able to run fast enough to get away from them? What if? What if? What if?

I realized there will always be "What ifs?" So, I changed the what ifs that I was thinking into:

What if I never actually allow myself to enjoy life again?

What if I remain a couch potato all my life in fear of moving forward?

What if I don't get to see all that my God has for me for fear of the what ifs?

And the big one....

What if God allowed me to live so that I can conquer what's on the other side of the "What ifs"?

Ahh...there are my wings! I can see them now. I can fly now. Even with a little fear, I can fly. God is my protector, my provider, and my security. He always has been and always will be.

I wanted a jeep so badly. I've wanted it since high school, but the specialists required a low car to install all of the equipment and such, so I was unable to get my Jeep. I had to get a small car. I wasn't pleased with it, but oh well, it'll do. At least I'm driving! Oh, I was driving from school to the grocery store, to my apartment, to church and more! No more fear! No more chains! The stroke couldn't hold me! I was on the road again! I acknowledged that growth. I acknowledged that blessing from God. The enemy wanted to blind me from seeing these things as blessings, but I see them!

Soon, I started feeling a piece of my previous life coming back. What a refreshing feeling! Even in my circumstances. What a refreshing feeling it is to once again be able to get up and go. To be able to feel freedom again and not be confined by some medical condition and prognosis.

This isn't how my story ends though.

On May 11, 2019, I walked across the stage at the University of Arkansas at Little Rock and claimed my Bachelor of Arts Degree in Sociology with a minor in Non-profit Management! I heard my name being called: *"Tichina Shonte Taylor"* as I walked across that stage while family from all over screamed and yelled. I saw my mother in that audience. I could feel her joy all the way across the room. My aunts and uncles, cousins, sisters, nieces and nephews were all there! Was this real? Was I a college graduate? Oh God! Did you really allow this day to come?

Through all the tears and all my fears; through all the rejections from the scholarships and the professors; through all the negative medical reports and the brain limitations and the physical limitations, I, God's Miracle Child had walked the stage and graduated with a bachelor's degree!

Miracles still happen. I'm a witness. This is one degree that I can proudly, humbly, and boldly say was *not* given to me! I earned every grade, every grade point average, and every accolade attached to my college degree! With tears streaming down my face and chills in my body, I say that I earned this degree with tears, sweat, faith, and a determination that was stirred up by the stroke that tried to hold me.

Eight years after graduating high school and seven years after suffering a major stroke that came to claim my life, I graduated college with a 3.0 grade point average, a Bachelor's degree in Sociology, a highly sought-after non-profit management certificate, and a faith that is unshakeable.

I have a college degree! That's yet another badge of miracles added to my life! I had to pay for my college classes, but it was worth it. I had to suffer more than the average Joe throughout my college career, but it was worth it. My brain has made *major* strides since the onset of the stroke. It's processing much better! I can do for myself; I can shop, cook, drive, read, write, and do things that normal people do. I have my own apartment, own car, and provide for myself. I may not be normal to the world, but I'm God's normal. I'm not ordinary, and that's okay because I'm God's extraordinary. "For God chooses the foolish things of the world to confound the wise" (1 Corinthians 1:27). Whatever may seem foolish to them as a result of my stroke, God took me and used my circumstances to confound, stun, confuse, and bewilder the wise. **I had a stroke, but I am not my stroke.**

Through all the tears and all my fears; through all the rejections, and limitations, I had walked the stage and graduated with a bachelor's degree!

I believe one day that I will walk straight again, but until then, I'm still walking.

Until God perfects my speech, I'm still talking.

Until God perfects my movement, I'm still moving.

Until God perfects my brain cells, I'm still thinking and processing.

Who knows? Maybe I'll be a stroke advocate one day. Maybe I'll be a speech pathologist helping others regain their ability to speak. Maybe

I'll be the social worker I always dreamed of.

Maybe one day, I will write and recite poems that inspire the world.

I am not what the doctors predicted.
I am not the stroke.
I am not the brain attack.
I am not the brain damage.

My name is Tichina Shonte Taylor, nicknamed Miracle since the day of my birth. My life is a series of miracles. I may not walk the way I used to, but I'm walking. I'm God's proof of miracles. I am a **walking** miracle.

Most Common Symptoms of Stroke

Source: Stroke.org [4]

- Sudden NUMBNESS or weakness of face, arm, or leg, especially on one side of the body
- Sudden CONFUSION, trouble speaking or understanding speech
- Sudden TROUBLE SEEING in one or both eyes
- Sudden TROUBLE WALKING, dizziness, loss of balance or coordination
- Sudden SEVERE HEADACHE with no known cause

May is National Stroke Awareness Month.

F FACE — Does one side of the face droop?

A ARM — Does one arm drift downward?

S SPEECH — Does the speech sound slurred or strange?

T TIME — If you observe any of these signs, call 911.

HEALTH JOURNAL

Taking care of your health is important and it starts with paying attention to your body and its messages. I included this journal for you. May God bless you.

Today's date: _____

Today I am feeling _____

_____

Symptoms _____

_____

_____

Doctor Notes _____

_____

_____

Today's date: _____

Today I am feeling _____

_____

Symptoms _____

_____

_____

Doctor Notes _____

_____

_____

Health Journal

Taking care of your health is important and it starts with paying attention to your body and its messages. I included this journal for you. May God bless you.

Today's date: _____

Today I am feeling _____

_____

Symptoms _____

_____

_____

Doctor Notes _____

_____

_____

Today's date: _____

Today I am feeling _____

_____

Symptoms _____

_____

_____

Doctor Notes _____

_____

_____

HEALTH JOURNAL

Taking care of your health is important and it starts with paying attention to your body and its messages. I included this journal for you. May God bless you.

Today's date: _____

Today I am feeling _____

_____

Symptoms _____

_____

_____

Doctor Notes _____

_____

_____

Today's date: _____

Today I am feeling _____

_____

Symptoms _____

_____

_____

Doctor Notes _____

_____

_____

HEALTH JOURNAL

Taking care of your health is important and it starts with paying attention to your body and its messages. I included this journal for you. May God bless you.

Today's date: _____

Today I am feeling _____

_____

Symptoms _____

_____

_____

Doctor Notes _____

_____

_____

Today's date: _____

Today I am feeling _____

_____

Symptoms _____

_____

_____

Doctor Notes _____

_____

_____

REFERENCES

1. Retrieved from http://www.strokecenter.org/patients/about-stroke/stroke-statistics

2. Retrieved from https://www.healthline.com/health/stroke/cerebral-ischemia

3. Retrieved from https://www.webmd.com/heart-disease/stroke

4. Retrieved from https://www.stroke.org/en/about-stroke/effects-of-stroke/emotional-effects-of-stroke/depression-and-stroke

About the Author

Tichina S. Taylor is a stroke survivor. She has achieved her Bachelor's Degree from the University of Arkansas at Little Rock. She is also a Certified Non-Profit Professional, among many other awards she has achieved from the University of Arkansas at Little Rock. She loves shopping and watching a good cinema movie at the theater. Tichina loves being around her family at functions and describes her family as one that puts a big smile on her face. You can reach her on Instagram @chinadoll7929.

About the Ghostwriter

Dr. Nioka Smith is a Licensed Clinical Christian Counselor, Marriage and Family Therapist-Advanced Certification, Published Author, Inspirational Speaker, and Licensed Educator. She is a well-established ghostwriter and is the President and CEO of J. Kenkade Publishing. Dr. Nioka Smith is the author of the book and workbook, "DIVAS Unchained: Women & Girls Breaking Free from Statistics & Strongholds." Her book has reached thousands of people in Canada, Jamaica, and all around the USA. She has a Bachelor's Degree in Speech Communication and Psychology, a Master's Degree in Education, and a Doctoral Degree in Christian Counseling. You can follow her on social media @drniokasmith.

J. Kenkade
PUBLISHING®

Also Available from
J. Kenkade Publishing

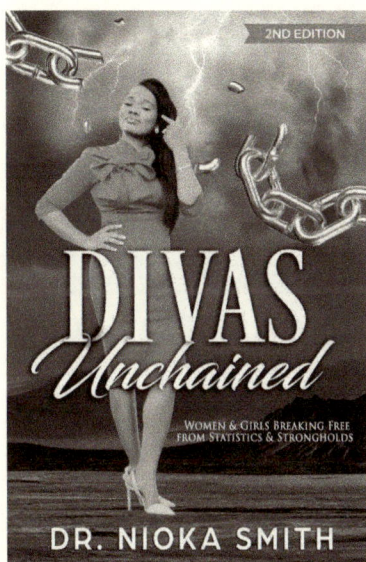

ISBN: 978-1-944486-25-9
Visit www.drniokasmith.com
Author: Dr. Nioka Smith

Sexually abused by her father at the age of 14, pregnant at the age of 17, and a nervous breakdown at the age of 28, Dr. Nioka Smith's painful past almost killed her, until the voice of the Lord guided her into destroying strongholds and reversing Satan's plan for her life. DIVAS Unchained is the powerful chain-breaking reality of the many unfortunate strongholds our women and girls face. Dr. Nioka uses her divine gift to help women and girls break free from destructive life cycles and prosper in all areas of life. Satan has lied to you. It's time to expose his lies. It's time to break free!

Also Available from
J. Kenkade Publishing

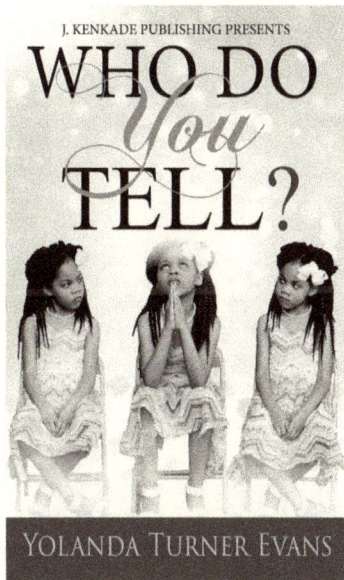

ISBN: 978-1-944486-37-2
Visit www.jkenkadepublishing.com
Author: Yolanda Turner Evans

Based on a real life story (the story of Yolanda Turner Evans) that made nationwide headline news. Yvette Diaz was violated and raped at the early age of nine by several family members. Feeling alone and unworthy as a teenager, she starts to look for love in all the wrong places. She has trudged through a long journey of hurt and pain and is the product of a deceased mother and absent father. She finally grows tired of running to survive and settling to keep the peace. She realizes that she's not a problem, but a solution to a world that was dying from the exact same thing she had experienced as a child.

Also Available from J. Kenkade Publishing

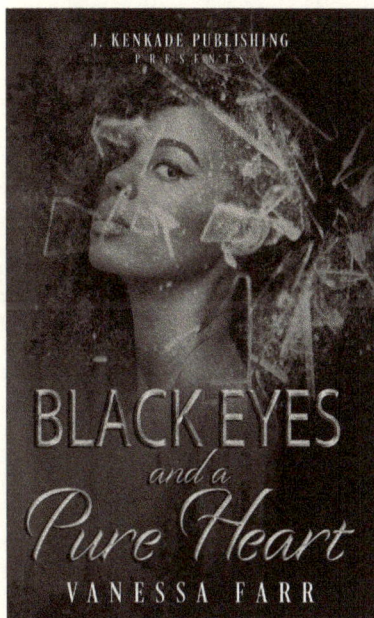

ISBN: 978-1-944486-23-5
Visit www.jkenkadepublishing.com
Author: Vanessa Farr

Black Eyes and a Pure Heart is a novel about the life of a young girl who must figure out how to live her life with a child at the age of 17. When the baby is born, her supportive spouse becomes an abusive predator. The black eyes represent the malicious nature of the domestic violence in the face of evil that so desperately tried to kill her. This short story reveals that the wrong path in life can gravely disfigure and blacken the eyes of young women and girls who seek easy pleasure.

Also Available from J. Kenkade Publishing

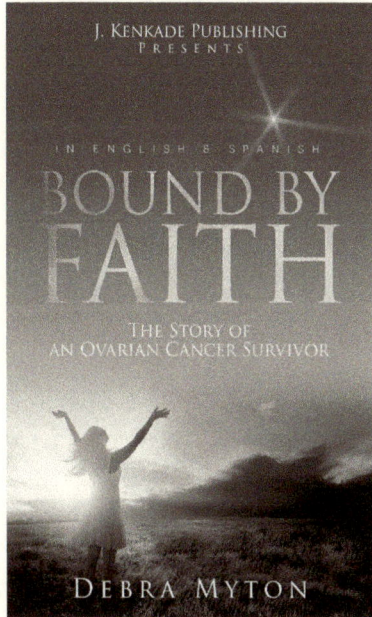

ISBN: 978-1-944486-20-4
Visit www.jkenkadepublishing.com
Author: Debra Myton

As the mother of two daughters, Debra became extremely concerned about her ovarian cancer diagnosis, nutrition, and weight loss. Research shows that people do not get second opinions about their health although health professionals do not see second opinions as a breach of trust from people. This book is a personal guide on how to handle any illness that a man or woman may face in life. This personal cancer story will make you laugh, cry, but overall, will empower you by faith. Join Debra in her journey of survival in "Bound by Faith".

www.ingramcontent.com/pod-product-compliance
Lightning Source LLC
LaVergne TN
LVHW041231080426
835508LV00011B/1150